WALT E. DISNEY
An Animated Life

Dona Herweck Rice

Consultant

Jamey Acosta, M.S.Ed
Reading Specialist and English Learner TOSA

Publishing Credits

Rachelle Cracchiolo, M.S.Ed., *Publisher*
Emily R. Smith, M.A.Ed., *SVP of Content Development*
Véronique Bos, *VP of Creative*
Robin Erickson, *Senior Art Director*

Image Credits: Cover, pp.7, 9, 11, 13, 15–21, 25, Alamy Stock Photo; pp.5, 23–24, Getty Images; p.8 Granger; p.10, Bettmann Archive via Getty Images; all other images from iStock or Shutterstock or in the public domain

Library of Congress Cataloging in Publication Control Number: 2024041784

5482 Argosy Avenue
Huntington Beach, CA 92649
www.tcmpub.com
ISBN 979-8-7659-9730-7

Table of Contents

Magic, Moxie, and a Mouse

The high-heel shoes many women wore sunk into the sticky asphalt, down the newly paved "Main Street." The bathroom plumbing worked well, but the drinking fountains did not. The rush to open required a decision to fix one or the other, since a local plumbers' **strike** ended just days before the opening. And while many invitations were handed out to a select group for the event, the raging **fervor** around the big day generated thousands of **counterfeit** tickets as well. Everyone wanted to be in Anaheim, California, on that hot July day in 1955. Disneyland was opening its gates for the first time, and the world would never be the same.

The truth is that's exactly what Walt Disney had planned all along.

Disneyland was the culmination of Walt Disney's dream. It was to be an **idealized** model of the country's past and a starry-eyed view of its future. All his life, Disney had been looking for a magical place where hope and happiness could take root. Disneyland was like a movie in which a person could step inside to experience life without the cares or concerns of the outside world. Disney—the man with the vision, the **moxie**, and the magic touch—was king there. And by his side, a little mouse held court.

Main Street, Marceline

Main Street, U.S.A., is the stretch of shops, restaurants, and early twentieth century carriages near Disneyland's entrance. This charming street's ambience is based on Disney's memory of his childhood hometown, Marceline, Missouri. He lived in Marceline with his family from 1906 to 1911.

Glossary

alter ego—an alternate personality or second self

ambience—the mood or feeling of a particular place

animated—a film made using a series of drawings or pictures

apprentice—employee in training to learn a profession

bankruptcy—a condition of financial failure brought about by not having the money to pay debts

commercial artist—a person who creates art for commercial, or business, purposes

communists—people who believe in a society in which the government owns the things that are used to make and transport products and in which there is no private property

counterfeit—made to look like a certain document in order to deceive

critical—as done by critics or reviewers

crude—very simple and basic

disparity—difference

distributor—a company that makes arrangements for a movie to be shown in various theaters

documentaries—movies based on factual records to inform or persuade

enlist—to register to join the armed forces

extrovert—a person with an outgoing personality who is energized by interactions with other people

fervor—high enthusiasm; frenzy

idealized—to think of or represent someone or something as being perfect

impish—playful and mischievous

labor union—an organization formed to protect the interests and rights of workers in a common trade or profession

laid off—released from employment

live action—done with live actors

moxie—courage and determination

solace—comfort

strike—a period of time in which workers stop working in an attempt to get employers to agree to worker demands

tangible—able to be felt

On July 17, 1955, 20,000 guests were invited on opening day, but 28,000 showed up!

The Boy

The century was young when Walter Elias Disney came into the world on December 5, 1901. He was the fourth son of Elias and Flora Disney, and he would be followed two years later by his only sister, Ruth. The family lived in Chicago, Illinois, where they had moved in 1889. Disney was born there.

Disney was an **extrovert** from the beginning. He had a big personality and a bigger imagination. From the time he was little, he wanted to make a name for himself. That was a hard thing to do in his family. Elias Disney was a stern father who expected his children to work hard for the good of the family. He was also a poor provider, frequently failing in business. The family often struggled to make ends meet.

Missouri Magic

A magical time arrived for Disney when the family moved to Missouri in 1906. For the few years they lived there during his childhood, Disney felt free and happy. He loved the natural world around the family farm, including the animals there. Also, railroad tracks were near his home, along which the Santa Fe Railroad traveled. The trains excited Disney and planted seeds in his imagination that would sprout years later.

Walt Disney

Big Brother, Roy

Roy Disney was born in 1893 and was eight years old when Walt Disney was born. Roy played a big role throughout Disney's life and was an important support for the man his little brother became.

Art School

Disney developed his skills by attending the Kansas City Art Institute for a few months. It was the only formal art training he would ever have.

An Artist's Heart

From his youngest days, Disney loved to draw. He craved approval, and his art skills helped to bring it. Art also gave Disney some **solace** at age nine, when the family left Marceline and moved to Kansas City. For the rest of his life, a piece of Disney would want to go back to Marceline, and his art would help him—in a **tangible** way—get there.

Disney worked hard to support his family and be the boy his father wanted him to be. For two years, he got up at 3:30 each morning before school to help his father deliver newspapers. At 17, Disney found an escape, although not an easy one. He joined the Red Cross Ambulance Corps and served as a driver in France right after World War I ended. He was too young to **enlist**, but Disney felt he "just had to get in there."

When Disney returned from France in 1919, he was just shy of 18. He had saved $500, and although he was meant to go to work in his father's jelly factory, he decided not to. He wanted to be an artist and get the world's attention. Although his parents were now in Chicago, Disney moved back to Kansas City, Missouri. He became a **commercial artist** with an advertising agency.

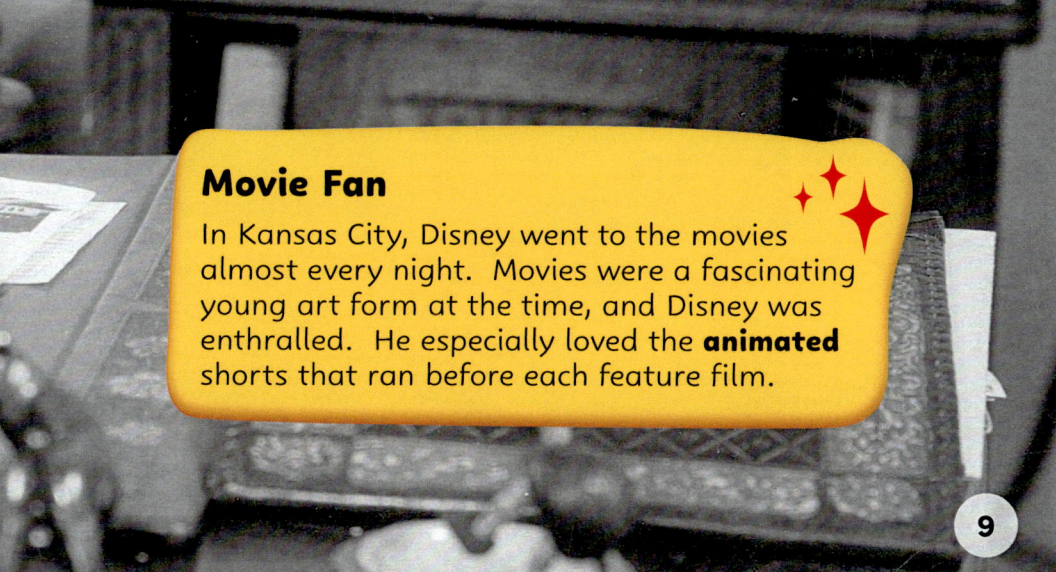

Movie Fan

In Kansas City, Disney went to the movies almost every night. Movies were a fascinating young art form at the time, and Disney was enthralled. He especially loved the **animated** shorts that ran before each feature film.

9

The Man

While working at the advertising agency, Disney met Ubbe "Ub" Iwerks. Disney and Iwerks became friends, and when they were **laid off**, both men went to work for the Kansas City Film Ad Company. It was there that Disney learned to animate.

In 1922, at just 20 years of age, Disney left the company and boldly started his own: Laugh-O-Gram Films. He hired four animators and one **apprentice** and set about making short cartoons for movie theaters. The company was offered a contract for six shorts, but once made, the **distributor** wouldn't pay the men. Disney struggled to pay his bills.

Helping Mom and Dad

During this time, Elias Disney's jelly factory failed. He and Flora moved to Kansas City to live with their sons. His father's presence put a damper on Disney's adventurous, risk-taking business style and his overall optimistic spirits.

Looking to make profitable animations, Disney turned to a combination of **live action** and animation. He made a series of shorts known as the Alice Comedies series, the first one called "Alice in Cartoon Land." The shorts starred a real girl in an animated world. During this financially trying time, Disney slept in his office and bathed at the train station. The work was good and the idea was a successful one, but it wasn't enough for Disney to avoid **bankruptcy**—a setback like his father experienced.

Virginia Davis played Alice in the Alice Comedies.

Learning from Felix

Competitors' animations during Disney's early days were generally **crude**. The stories were often driven by violent gags. Pat Sullivan, creator of Felix the Cat, stood out from the crowd. Felix is a bit of a troublemaker but good-hearted. Disney studied Sullivan's work intently.

On to Los Angeles

In July 1923, Disney hopped on a train to Los Angeles, California. Despite being nearly broke, Disney purchased a first-class ticket. He knew that somehow, someway, he was onto something big. He intended to be a movie director in Hollywood's growing film industry.

Disney tried to get hired at various movie studios, but he couldn't make it happen. His brother Roy had moved to Los Angeles and was selling vacuum cleaners—a job he tried to convince Disney to do as well. Disney was considering it when he received a telegram from New York distributor M. J. Winkler, who was interested in Disney's Alice Comedies. She would pay $1,500 each for 12 of the shorts. Disney talked Roy into working with him. Roy would manage the finances and raise funds, while Disney would come up with the ideas and manage the art. They called their company Disney Brothers Cartoon Studio.

Walt Disney (fourth from left), his animators, and the Alice actress either in late 1926 or early 1927

The new venture brought success to the brothers. They built houses on adjoining lots and married their sweethearts. Lillian Bounds was an inker in Disney's company who found her boss to be dynamic and great fun. They married in July 1925. The next February, Disney moved the studio and gave it a new name. He was the idea man who made everything happen, so the company became The Walt Disney Studios.

Walt Disney and Lillian Bounds

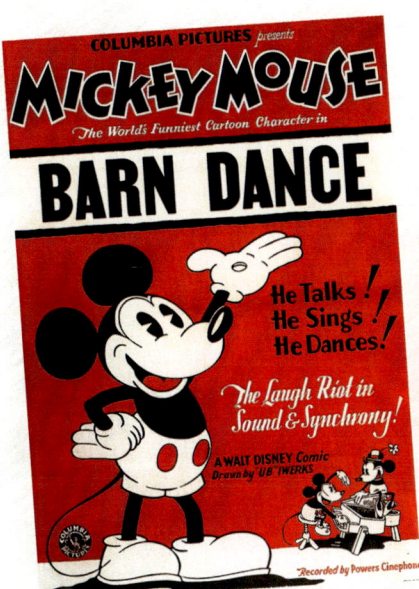

Ub to the Rescue!

Disney knew he wasn't a strong enough artist for the new company. He turned to his old friend Ub Iwerks to create what he could not. This is an example of Iwerk's art.

The Mouse

To achieve the success he craved, Disney decided that creating an animated character should be his next venture. Together with Iwerks, Disney thought about Felix the Cat and other popular characters of the time. *How about a rabbit?* he wondered. Iwerks drew while Disney wrote, and Oswald the Lucky Rabbit was born. The humorous character was a quick success.

Disney Studios worked out a contract with M. J. Winkler and her new husband, producer Charles Mintz, for 26 episodes featuring Oswald. Disney now employed many animators, and business was booming. But most of the animators weren't happy. Disney took much of the profits and credit. He inspired the animators to do great work, but he also drove them to work incredibly hard without much personal benefit.

In the meantime, Mintz realized that through Disney's carelessness in their contract, Mintz and Winkler owned the rights to Oswald. Mintz convinced many of Disney's animators to come work for them in New York. Oswald went with them. Only loyal Iwerks, while sought by Mintz, remained with Disney.

In 1928, Disney traveled by train to New York to seek a new contract and keep business alive, but all seemed lost.

Mintz/Muntz
Charles Muntz, a villain in Disney Pixar's 2009 animated film *Up,* is said to have been based on Charles Mintz.

It's...Mortimer?

Unlike his father, whose spirits were crushed under many losses, Disney chose to strive on. He gathered Roy, Iwerks, and a few others to brainstorm a new, better character. Once again, Iwerks drew while Disney developed the personality. *How about a mouse?* Disney wondered this time. The mouse was **impish**, playful, and no matter what, always a winner. Disney thought of him as his **alter ego**. He wanted to name the mouse Mortimer, but Lillian had a better idea: Mickey Mouse. One of America's most recognized and beloved icons was born.

At first, there was little interest in the new character. But Disney decided to add sound effects (including his own voice as Mickey's) and music to his animation to help tell the story. Theaters would need advanced sound systems to play his new animations, and it took months to get distributors.

Then, on November 11, 1928, Mickey Mouse made his debut in "Steamboat Willie," which started a two-week run at New York's Colony Theater. Audiences loved him! Some viewers asked theater owners to delay the main feature and play the cartoon again. People even started a Mickey Mouse Club! Just like that, Mickey Mouse and Walt Disney were international sensations.

Number of Disney Shorts by Decade

1920s	102
1930s	184
1940s	159
1950s	94
1960s	14
1970s	2
1980s	7
1990s	8
2000s	6
2010s	8
2020s	3*

*as of this book's printing

The Movies

With his new celebrity, Disney worked harder than ever. But it took its toll. He relentlessly watched over every inch of animation his company produced. He nervously smoked and drummed his fingers on tables. When Lillian suffered from health issues, Disney became deeply depressed and worked even harder. Finally, his doctor insisted he stop all work and take a long vacation. That's just what he did.

Disney returned from vacation a new man. He was reenergized. A period of inspiration began, filled with cutting-edge ideas. First up, Disney Studios created Silly Symphonies, which cost a fortune to make but took animation to levels never before reached. It became a true art form. To create this art, Disney grew his staff to more than 200 artists.

Silly Symphonies

Silly Symphonies were animated shorts that were set to music. The cartoon characters danced and moved in time with the music.

Advancing the Art

Disney wanted to do everything he could to advance the art of animation. He offered his artists high-level drawing classes. He brought live animals and dancers to the studio for them to study. He even offered acting classes so animators could fully understand how to make the characters come alive. He gave them room to experiment. Disney did everything he could to support his top artists and make them feel like a family—his family.

Boys' Club

Many women worked for Disney but only in support positions. All his top artists and close staff were men. In fact, Disney called them "his boys." There was also great **disparity** among his staff. Top artists were treated and paid very well, but the rest earned very low wages and received little credit for their work.

Snow White

Soon, a new inspiration consumed Disney. He wanted to make the first feature-length cartoon. He wanted it to be a realistic and story-driven work of art. The film would make audiences laugh and cry.

The movie budget multiplied six times, and the staff swelled to 600 throughout production. Artists worked long days to meet the strict release date Disney had set: December 21, 1938. The animators faced a difficult job. To make the movie, each hand-drawn, inked, and painted cel had to be shot on film. The last cel of the film wasn't even painted until November 27. There were 24 frames per second of film and multiple cels per frame. And the final movie included 200,000 cels! The task seemed impossible. Even so, *Snow White and the Seven Dwarfs* was released on time to huge **critical** acclaim.

Strike!

The Screen Cartoonists Guild, a labor union formed in the late 1930s, was soon in every studio but Disney's. Employee dissatisfaction and disputes with Disney led to a massive strike in 1941. Roy ended the strike in the employees' favor while Disney was on vacation.

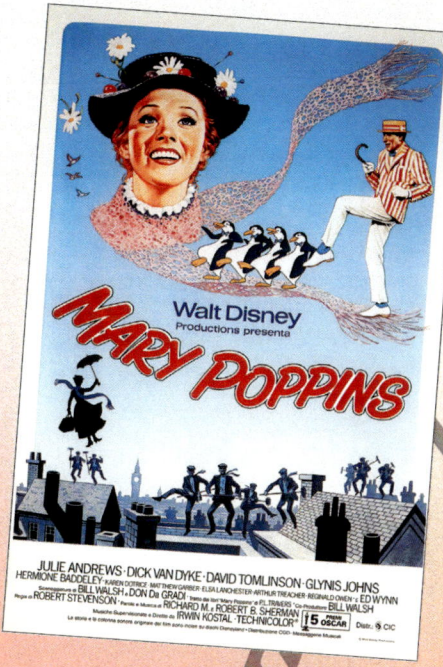

Other highly acclaimed films followed *Snow White*, but each one was financially draining. To keep the company afloat, the early films were followed by simpler animations, live-action movies, and nature **documentaries**.

Disney's movie masterpiece was filmed in 1963 and released the following year. He combined animation and live action once again in the musical film *Mary Poppins*. It is the only film produced by Disney himself to be nominated for the Academy Award® for Best Picture.

The Red Scare

Disney was dismayed that his staff felt overworked, underpaid, and unappreciated. He was sure that **communists** were behind the labor union and were turning his staff against him. He testified in Congress against union leaders who he believed were communist organizers.

The Happiest Place on Earth

As Disney's film business flourished, a new inspiration took hold. He had long wanted to create a safe place for families to enjoy themselves. Disney had recently built a massive studio in Burbank. Next to his studio, he built a new company called WED Enterprises (for Walter Elias Disney). There, he and the WED team worked on a new dream. It would be a fantasy world for people to visit and escape reality. Disney called it Disneyland.

Before Disneyland, amusement parks were rough, dirty, and not always safe. Disneyland would be the ultimate family destination. Everything would be clean, safe, and family friendly. The park would capture the imagination. But Disney needed money to make it happen. Roy worked a deal with ABC television to produce a weekly show during which Disney would talk about the planned park and share stories inspired by it. In exchange for the show, *Walt Disney's Disneyland*, ABC gave Disney the money he needed to build his magical land.

Disney finally had his utopia! He even built an apartment above the Main Street fire station where he and Lillian could stay. Disney spent a great deal of time at Disneyland. His desk overlooked Main Streets, where he worked, and surveyed the kingdom that he—and a little mouse—had built.

Rush to Completion

Disney wanted construction of Disneyland to be complete in one year. Because of this rush, with just six weeks to opening, fewer than half the attractions were ready. The iconic centerpiece, Sleeping Beauty's castle, was far from complete. Even so, the not-quite-complete park opened on schedule and was a success beyond anyone's imagination.

Marceline to the Rescue

Returning from a trip to New York in 1946, Disney stopped in his hometown, Marceline. He was reinspired by how idyllic it appeared to him and what he felt there as a child. The seeds that had been planted in his imagination during childhood were nurtured a little more on this stop. In just a few months, they would begin to bloom.

Sleeping Beauty's Castle on opening day, 1955

Disneyland in the Beginning

Through television, Disney introduced audiences each week to a different area of the planned park and the places and stories that inspired each one. Although Disneyland has changed since then, much of the original plan remains. The park started with five key areas that explored America's past and future, world travels, and favorite Disney stories.

Disney intentionally left out an area of the park focused on the present-day world. Disney wanted guests to leave their real lives behind when they entered his world. In fact, aircraft and drones are not permitted over Disneyland and for a few miles outside its perimeters. This agreement is meant, in part, to preserve the fantasy within Disneyland that Disney hoped to create. The park was created as a fantasy come to life.

Adventureland

Main Street, U.S.A.

Frontierland

Tomorrowland

Fantasyland

A Land for Everything

Each of the five lands when Disneyland opened were geared toward a particular theme. Frontierland was based on pioneer days and the Old West. Fantasyland was based on some of Disney's animated films. Tomorrowland was envisioned as a hoped-for future. Adventureland was inspired by the jungles of Africa and Asia. And Main Street, U.S.A., was modeled after Disney's childhood town, Marceline, Missouri.

The Rest of the Story

One million visitors came to Disneyland in its first 10 weeks. Millions upon millions have visited since. But Disneyland was not the end of Disney's dreaming. In the 1960s, he began to plan the Experimental Prototype Community of Tomorrow, or EPCOT. Disney bought 27,000 acres (almost 11,000 hectares) of land in Florida on which to build his ideal community.

Unfortunately, Disney never saw EPCOT as he had dreamed. A lifelong smoker, Disney was diagnosed with lung cancer in the fall of 1966. On December 14, while in the hospital, he urgently relayed his plans to Roy. He wanted his brother to oversee the EPCOT he envisioned. Disney died that night, December 14, 1966. He was 65, and his final dream was unfulfilled.

But the dream lived on under Roy's leadership. It became Walt Disney World, a thriving theme park, hotel, and entertainment compound. Additional Disney amusement parks have since been built in Asia and Europe. Millions of people visit these parks each year.

Disney movies, merchandise, amusement parks, and more are hugely popular, and the Disney brand is one of the world's strongest. The man and the mouse are legendary. Disney grew up wanting to make a name for himself. Some might argue that he made *the* name for himself—the most recognizable and beloved name of the twentieth century. Disney, once the boy with big dreams, has become a name for the ages.

Front-Page News

Newspapers around the world carried the story of Disney's death on their front pages. Disney was an international superstar, and the whole world mourned his passing.

EPCOT

EPCOT is one of four theme parks in Walt Disney World. It is made of two lands, or areas, including Future World (where future technology is studied) and World Showcase (where countries and cultures are explored). Disney's original idea for EPCOT, which did not come to be, was for it to be a live-in community. It was to have had apartments, houses, and a climate-controlled "city center," including a hotel, shopping, restaurants, and more.

PICTURE SPOT

Dream It!

You have the opportunity to design and open your own amusement park. Think about what you have learned from this book as well as theme parks you have visited.

- Where will your park be located? What will you name it? Will you have one theme throughout the park? You want many people to visit, so think through these questions thoroughly!

- Create and name at least five rides you want to include. What other offerings will there be in the park? Food and drinks? Shows or films?

- Sketch the layout. Yours may include rides, restaurants, theaters, restrooms, and other facilities that will be necessary to run your park.

- Provide a written explanation of each ride along with your reason for the choice of name. You might also want to include descriptions of the restaurants and/or other facilities.

- You may complete the drawing and writing by hand, by computer, or a combination of both.

Index

Try It!

You can create a short animation of your own without any technology involved.

- Make a little booklet by cutting several sheets of 8.5 × 11 inch (22 × 28 centimeter) paper each into 16 small rectangles of the same size. Stack the sheets, and staple them together as shown.

- Starting with the last page, draw a simple figure on the side of the paper away from the stapled edge.

- On the sheet before that one, draw the figure again, but this time with its position slightly different. Continue in this way up through all the pages. The drawings will show the figure in movement, such as taking steps or taking off into flight.

- Hold the booklet on the stapled edge and flip through the pages quickly from back to front. The animation comes to life!